Freshwater Fly-Fishing

Tips from the Pros

MARK D. WILLIAMS

A FIRESIDE BOOK
PUBLISHED BY SIMON & SCHUSTER

FIRESIDE
Rockefeller Center
1230 Avenue of the Americas
New York, NY 10020

Copyright © 1998 by Mark D. Williams

Designed by Guenet Abraham

Manufactured in the United States of America

1   3   5   7   9   10   8   6   4   2

Library of Congress Cataloging-in-Publication Data
Williams, Mark D., date.
Freshwater fly-fishing : tips from the pros /
Mark D. Williams.
p.   cm.
"A Fireside Book."
1. Fly-fishing. I. Title.
SH456.W524   1998
799.1'24—dc21   98-3377   CIP
ISBN 0-684-84253-X (alk. paper)

I dedicate this book

to my father,

Gary Williams.

His strong silence, hard work, success,

and dedication to a spiritual life provided

me with a model of what every son

should strive to become.

Contents

Techniques

∘∘∘ **1** ∘∘∘

Dead-drifting a streamer like a Green Ghost or one of Bud Wilcox's Kennebago Smelt patterns is another effective means of enticing those tight-lipped landlocks. The tails of pools are an excellent spot to try this trick.

∘∘∘ **2** ∘∘∘

Work the streamer through the current as you normally would, but instead of stripping back in when the streamer swings, let out some slack and allow the fly to drift back with the slower current into the deadwater. Watch your line carefully, and be ready for a vicious strike when you do finally begin to strip your line.

BOB NEWMAN

°°° **3** °°°

So many anglers today are enamored of beadhead nymphs. To more closely imitate the underwater action of a nymph, use unweighted nymphs and bring the fly down with splitshot on the leader. The nearly weightless nymph will dance in the current in a much more lifelike fashion than one weighted otherwise. Keep the splitshot just a few inches from the fly despite your fear of the trout being spooked by a foreign object that close to the fly. The trout could really care less.

They live in an environment filled with tumbling gravel and streambed debris. If they ignored every nymph that came downstream next to a bit of drifting gravel, they would soon starve to death.

RALPH AND LISA CUTTER

∘∘∘ **4** ∘∘∘

Put a small pile of desiccant powder such as Seidel's dry fly crystal in the palm of your hand and scrub your nymph with it. The nymph will now be impervious to water and will tightly retain a glistening air bubble as so many aquatic insects do.

RALPH AND LISA CUTTER

∘∘∘ **5** ∘∘∘

Fly-fishing small streams requires a discipline uncommon to larger rivers, leaving many anglers holding their heads low, cursing the hike in and out. Small-stream fishing means casting to spooky trout in clear water in tight conditions. Anglers fishing small streams often suffer scratched arms, scraped knees, bruised egos. I fish small streams for a living and have found the following tactics effective:

Use the Closer-Lower method—the closer you approach the water, the lower to the ground you must be.

Your footfalls will scare fish. Move slowly, walk softly.

Find cover behind boulders, trees, and their shadows.

Keep your shadow from looming over the water.

Keep your rod parallel to the ground with the tip behind you.

Show your rod only when you are ready to cast. Keep the rod's shadow off the water.

Use the longest and lightest tippet/leader combination possible.

Delicate presentations and drag-free drifts are a must.

Employ nontraditional casts to present your fly: roll, sidearm, bow-and-arrow, and dap.

Wade as little as possible.

Take your time.

DOC THOMPSON

∘∘∘ **6** ∘∘∘

The sun can be your best friend or your worst enemy. Did you ever notice while fishing with the sun in front of you that your results were poor? And fishing the same water at another time of day brought excellent results? It could be that the sun was reflecting off your rod or other equipment and alerting the fish.

Fishing with the sun behind you not only gives you the best chance to see the fish but allows you to get closer without the fish seeing you. I plan my fishing day to coincide with the sun's position, to minimize my reflection. By the same token, with the sun somewhat behind me, I am on the blind side of the fish. Use some common sense and just be careful that your shadow does not alert the fish.

ED SHENK

○○○ **7** ○○○

Your topographical map is a real friend when you are searching for off-the-beaten-path places to fly-fish. I often hear complaints that Montana is getting too crowded and I have to admit that there is some crowding on the "name" rivers. On the other hand, there are literally thousands of miles of ignored waters in this state (and many other states). I use a topo map to find them. The books of maps from DeLorme are my sources of choice.

What I look for when I am researching for a new fly-fishing prospect is a stream that is a tributary to a famous body of water—a river or lake. From there, I look for a foot trail or unimproved road access. The more difficult the access, the fewer the anglers.

Use the topo-map approach in conjunction with state fishing regulations books. Included in most regs books are lists of waters and the fish they contain.

AL BEATTY

∘∘∘ **8** ∘∘∘

Early in the season, the fish in the larger western rivers are close to the bank. As the season progresses and the water levels start dropping, the fish begin to disperse. By the time August arrives, the fish are scattered throughout the whole river.

While floating these western rivers after the water has dropped, look for the darker areas in the current. They signal the deeper holding water. Those areas may be as small as a foot square or could be several square feet, but they are where the fish are located. Cast a hopper or stimulator pattern at the head of the "dark areas" and wait for the explosion.

AL BEATTY

ooo **9** ooo

Fishing spring creeks, like Montana's Depuy's, Armstrong's, or Nelson's, can be extremely difficult. If you run into a day when the fish are actively feeding and they ignore all of your offerings, try this tip.

Search the creek for a spot along the banks where a willow branch is sticking down into the water and vegetation has collected, forming a floating pad. This is where the big trout hide. The ones you spot in the middle of the creek are usually the smaller fish.

AL BEATTY

ooo **10** ooo

When you have located a floating weed pad in a spring creek, watch it closely. The big trout living there only stick their noses from under it less than half an inch to select a food item floating by. Because the rise form is almost nonexistent, it is hard to see them, so you must pay attention. Once you spot a weed-pad feeder, move slightly upstream from the trout and present your fly on a slack-line downstream dead-drift. Your pattern must pass within an inch of the edge of the floating pad to be in the fish's window of vision.

AL BEATTY

∘∘∘ **11** ∘∘∘

If the water is low, as it often is in late summer and early fall, anglers need to remember that the fish will be especially spooky. This calls for stalking—tread lightly when approaching the riverbank. Keep a low profile. Try fishing from your knees. Fish on your stomach if you must. Remember that if the fish see you or your shadow, the game is over.

HARRY MURRAY

∘∘∘ **12** ∘∘∘

Fish across broken water like riffles because they consider this kind of habitat protective.

HARRY MURRAY

∘∘∘ **13** ∘∘∘

Once you've found a potential holding spot, here are a few ways to deliver your fly. Drift the fly with or without Action—try both methods. Work your fly by throwing it into crosscurrents. Work it up and down the merge line of currents.

MARK KOVACH

∘∘∘ **14** ∘∘∘

The majority of streams in the Rocky Mountains are the antithesis of the English water where fly-fishing and its time-honored techniques originated. Ballet-movement casts that gently unfurl over 50 feet of water are suitable for the unflappable currents of the Yorkshire countryside. But in pocket water, where water hurls itself over rocks and melts around dozens of rounded granite boulders, a classic cast is as worthless as an American big-brewery lager in a London pub.

If you lay your fly line across complex currents, where fast- and slow-moving water lie in alternating bands on the surface, it will instantly drag the fly in a most unnatural manner. The trick to fishing such water is to hold as much of the fly line off the water as possible, keeping your leader and the fly in a single-speed current lane.

On mountain waters you need to use your rod not as a spring-loaded launcher but as a long arm to place your fly in the proper current lane or in a likely pocket. It doesn't look like traditional fly-fishing, and it's actually a whole lot easier.

Take advantage of the trout's poor visibility in choppy currents to get up close to your target. Using your long arm, simply reach across the water and drop your leader into the proper feeding lane. Or, with a flip of the forearm, make a short, punching stroke to guide the fly to the target. Then, with your rod held high, keep only the leader and at most a few feet of line on the water. A short float in the right place is all you need. Use your rod tip to control the line.

Lift, drop, or twist your arm, perhaps adding a full-body lean to keep your line off the water and the fly moving on target. Drag the fly slightly to make small adjustments to the float before the fly reaches the target lie. Watch carefully for the strike. By keeping your "casts" short and your fly line off the water, you'll have Fredric Halford turning in his grave but more trout on the end of your line.

CRAIG MARTIN

∘∘∘ **15** ∘∘∘

Wade Fishing with Nymphs or Wet Flies in Fast Pocket Water.

Your position relative to the pocket is most critical to the proper tight line drift. It is always tempting, especially in wading fast water, to try to cast a weighted nymph into a promising pocket without moving into the proper position. In many fast-water pockets there is only one position, relative to the pocket, that will allow you to shorten your line and drift the nymph properly with a tight line and no drag. You must learn to read the water, know where in the hole the strikes are likely to occur, and move to the right position below the pocket.

Approach the pocket from downstream (always), get into position to use as short a line as possible without disturbing the fish by your proximity. When you reach that position, wait quietly for half a minute or so while you solidify your footing and determine the proper cast. Remember, the first cast is critical. Drop the nymph at or above the the head of the pocket where the current will allow the nymph to sink before drifting through the critical part of the pocket. The nymph should drift near the bottom along the shear (seam) between the quiet water and the fast current that forms the pocket. Keep your line tight; this first cast will likely bring a hard strike. Be ready.

If you have not positioned yourself properly with respect to the pocket, your first and most critical cast will probably drag your nymph and alert the trout. Above all, do not make that first cast until you are certain that you can do so drag-free. If you are going to get any action in that pocket, a well placed/drifted first cast will bring you a strike about 50 percent of the time.

DAN POWELL

○○○ **16** ○○○

If you're used to small water, don't be intimidated the first time you fish a truly big river. Sure, wading the heavy flow is going to be a challenge, and you'll probably have to deal with more wind, but trout are trout—pretty much. Break the big water into small pieces, and look for fish in the same places you've found them before, near current seams, where the depth changes—in other words, where's there's shelter from the current and a reliable food supply.

JIM BUTLER

○○○ **17** ○○○

Whenever I approach a stream, I always start casting from 10 feet away (bankside vegetation permitting). I learned long ago (and the hard way, many times) that big trout are often right up near the bank, even in very shallow water. So I resist the urge to just march up to the water's edge and start casting to that good-looking riffle out in the middle of the stream.

Instead, I stand on dry ground and plop my fly, wet or dry, right at the edge of the water. Then I lengthen the cast a few feet, then a few feet more. Only when I've thoroughly covered the water right by the bank do I start to wade.

Try it. You'll be surprised how many fish you'll start picking up . . . and you'll wonder how many fish you've spooked over the years by not fishing the stream edge first!

JAY CASSELL

∘∘∘ **18** ∘∘∘

We don't have time to apply the principle of resting the water anymore, especially on the more popular tailwater fisheries where the next guy is waiting in line to fish. But when you can, give a good spot a rest now and again after you have thoroughly covered the water. Just sit on the bank, exercise your patience, watch the birds and observe the water. Often, after you're sure the fishing has tailed off, you'll be surprised by renewed fish activity.

STEPHEN TRAMMEL

ooo **19** ooo

Segmented Presentation

One way to increase your potential for getting a strike by up to ten times is to break your presentations into segments. Any section of stream can be segmented, even long runs and glides. Of course, your segment presentations will be only as short as the fish allow.

Make short drifts over segments of the stream where you suspect the fish to be holding. Start your drift two feet or so above the lie and pick up the drift about the same distance below the lie. This gives you a 4-foot precise drift over a fish. If you had made a usual drift, the long drift we are taught to employ, say 40 feet instead, your control over the line and the fly suffer.

In the same amount of time you could have drifted the 40-foot presentation, you could have placed your fly over the 4-foot segment ten times, ten more opportunities for a strike. With the shorter distance, your drift is much more controllable, allowing you to make careful adjustments and a variety of floats.

BARRIE BUSH

∘∘∘ **20** ∘∘∘

Line Control

Getting strikes depends on three things: Presentation, presentation, presentation. The most common fault I observe as a guide is that most fly-fishers use too much line, and this mistake makes for repeated poor presentations. Focus on the objective of making tightly controlled drifts.

Lots of line on the water interferes with meticulous management of the drift, mending and setting the hook. Precise accuracy is less likely with long casts. In-air adjustments are less effective. Back-cast clearance is a problem. Keep your line short, and compensate for being closer to your targets by carefully locating yourself in optimum casting positions.

BARRIE BUSH

∘∘∘ **21** ∘∘∘

Timing the Mend

I frequently see fly-fishers having trouble making an effective mend in their line during the drift because they wait too long to make the mend stroke. Try making your mend a little earlier and you should find it easier and more effective.

BARRIE BUSH

∘∘∘ **22** ∘∘∘

Swing and Rise

When drifting a nymph, be sure to allow the line to tighten at the end of the drift. This causes the fly to swing across the current and rise toward the surface. Then let it rest in the current for a few seconds.

This technique simulates an emerging or panicked insect and can often cause a strike.

BARRIE BUSH

∘∘∘ **23** ∘∘∘

In heavily fished rivers, where the local folks throw back everything but the stocker trout, and the ultralight and modern crowd tend to exhaust game fish beyond recovery, northern pike, very large brown trout, big stripers and others, will move just downstream of these anglers for easy meals, castoffs, and trash.

By positioning yourself across and slightly downstream from just such a location, you can cast a large bait-fish-type streamer across and slightly upstream (5 degrees across) then mend your line downstream to make it sink. You can also mend the line upstream to keep the fly near the surface, leading your fly out and away from the opposite bank, perfectly replicating your predator's next stunned meal.

JERRAL DERRYBERRY

∘∘∘ **24** ∘∘∘

Through pure luck, I discovered this technique. It seems to be very productive when all else fails. Let out 20 to 30 feet of line. Let your line, leader, and fly float downstream until all slack is out. Point your rod downstream, turn around and walk upstream for a bit. You will be amazed at the number of strikes you will get. The combination of the fly pushing against the current and the rod tip bumping up and down makes the fly act life-like. Hold on to your rod, because the action can get fast and furious.

Tom Theus

∘∘∘ **25** ∘∘∘

Many anglers are confident that the most effective means to fish for bass is a spin-tackle affair, best left to those armed with Ambassador reels and the latest space-age technology rod breakthrough. Here are three things I have discovered firsthand, fishing right next to the spinmeisters.

1. When the sky is high blue, a front is upon you and the fish are not feeding aggressively, an angler with a fly-rod can strum your head. The ability of the fly-fisher to control the speed of the retrieve while adding motion from the stripping hand can be deadly.

2. A long-rodder who can cast worth his salt can consistently hit closer to the weed line, the hot spot for bass-in-waiting. Fly-fishers can often get more casts to the strike zones quicker than anglers with spin-casting gear because they don't have to take the time to reel in 25 feet of line. They simply pick up, cast, and place the fly in the zone.

3. Under normal conditions, the fly-fisher who leaves his or her fly in the strike zone longer and slower will catch more fish.

RAY SASSER

∘∘∘ **26** ∘∘∘

Two basic tips when nymphing: (1) keep your line off the water by lifting and adjusting your rod tip. This will help you set the hook quicker; and (2) if you see a flash under the water, lift your rod because you've got a strike; he's on your fly.

ED ADAMS

∘∘∘ **27** ∘∘∘

Better Hopper Fishing

One of my favorite times of the year to fish is when the grasshoppers are active. In New Mexico, thanks to our warm consistent weather, this can be from early summer through late fall. My favorite "hopper" stream is the Rio Penasco, a small spring creek in southern New Mexico. When the hoppers are "on," it is not unusual to see double-digit browns throw caution to the wind and actively rise to an imitation. You may have heard that when fishing hopper patterns, it is extremely effective to aim your forward cast straight into the water next to the bank, so as to cause a loud splash. Trout that have focused their attention on terrestrials expect such a commotion and thus are attracted to the sound. Strikes can often be savage, and often take the angler by surprise.

The problem with fishing hoppers in this manner is that between the splash casting and the savage strikes, even the best deer hair hopper patterns don't retain their floating capabilities for very long. To remedy this problem, try using hopper patterns tied with foam bodies. If you can't find them at your local fly shop, you can purchase Rainy's float foam in various colors (I like yellow) and use the enclosed instructions to tie your own. Once you try some of these patterns, you will be amazed at how high they float and the amount of dunking they can take. You'll be able to really smash the flies into the edges of undercut banks time and time again without worrying about sinking flies.

Chances are you will catch more and bigger fish too. You can also purchase foam in stone-fly colors, in order to tie another extremely effective foam imitation.

MANUEL MONASTERIO

∘∘∘ **28** ∘∘∘

If you have ever fished a beaver pond, you know how skittish the trout can be. Common sense and all the experts will tell you to tie on long, fine tippets, attach micro-flies, cast delicately, and leave the fly motionless for a few minutes in order to trick the trout. To this I say, "Hogwash."

That finesse approach might work for many, but I have used my clumsy power approach on numerous beaver ponds and find that the only consistent method to catch beaver-pond residents is a technique I discovered years ago by accident. If I am not catching fish, I like to tie on big flies. At least I can see the fly not catching any trout.

One day up in the Lake Fork Gunnison Valley, at a complex of beaver ponds, I was having difficulty getting the brookies to rise to the small caddisflies I was using, so I tied on a Mathews X-Caddis, a big one. I tossed it into the middle of the pond splat! on top the pod of feeding fish. They scattered. So I started stripping the fly back to shore. The strike was so hard the fly broke off.

I caught over twenty fish from that pond that day. And every pond I fish, I find this weird pattern where the trout attack my large stripped flies. I have also found this technique works well on small, high country lakes.

I like flies with rubber legs, sizes 6 to 12. I don't use light tippet, since the strikes are so fierce. This technique is deadly when cast to rising trout—toss the fly over the rise form and start stripping. The speed of retrieve and motion varies from time to time but the end result is always the same.

KEN MEDLING

○○○ **29** ○○○

It is almost impossible to make a "bad" cast as long as you can put the fly beyond the first fish. The first thing the fish sees is the fly rather than the line, leader, or any knots. Whenever possible, get above the fish, cast down and across stream, then drag the fly into the current lane immediately above the fish. Drop the rod tip and feed slack so the fly rides drag-free with the current to the fish.

Set the hook by allowing the fish to take the fly and go under with a slightly slack line, In this way, the fly will almost always stick in the tip of the mouth or in the corner of the jaw.

BOB NEWMAN

∘∘∘ **30** ∘∘∘

Trout spook easier during low-water conditions, so special techniques are needed. When casting to trout in low water, you will want to avoid all commotion. Keep yourself low to the ground. False-cast *off* the water to get distance. Cast only when you have correct distance and accuracy. Use a sidearm motion if the overhead tip can be seen by fish. Try to drop your line on the bank or moss rather on the water to avoid splashing.

HARTT WIXOM

∘∘∘ **31** ∘∘∘

One of the most overlooked aspects of fishing streams is where you put your big, fat feet. You must know where to stand in order to properly cast, to get a good float and to cover enough water.

HARRY MURRAY

∘∘∘ **32** ∘∘∘

If you are a more capable caster, make longer casts down and across. Use a lighter and longer tippet. The longer and lighter the tippet, the more strikes you will get.

HARRY MURRAY

ooo **33** ooo

Try to be graceful. Hold the fly-rod as if it were a live sparrow. For short casts, use short strokes. For long casts, use long strokes. For longer casts, use a longer casting stroke. Think of a heavier application of power, not a quicker one. Strive for a harder stop.

MEL KRIEGER

ooo **34** ooo

For good loops, stop the rod tip at the end of each casting stroke. For tailing loops and tangled leaders, use a longer casting stroke. Keep the bend in the rod longer. Think *smooth, continuous, oily* during the casting stroke. *Sling* the line.

MEL KRIEGER

∘∘∘ **35** ∘∘∘

If you often fish pools and tailouts and flats—smooth water—for rising trout, the single thing you can learn that will improve your catch the most is the downstream, slack-line wiggle cast.

DAVE HUGHES

∘∘∘ **36** ∘∘∘

When choosing a rod, think about the kind of fishing you do and the water you frequent. Most of all, choose a *fishing* rod, not just a *casting* rod. It's fine if your 5-weight can boom out 70 feet of line and turn over a 14-foot leader in the process, but can you also place a Blue-Wing Olive 25 feet from where you stand—with accuracy? You'll need that kind of performance a lot more often than you'll need the casting-pool heroics.

A corollary: When you practice your casting, work on hitting targets close to you; don't just concentrate on stretching your entire fly-line across your lawn.

JIM BUTLER

Get Close

Trout can be approached quite closely in pocket water. The swirling currents restrict vision through the surface and the rushing water masks wading noise. Advantages of getting close to a suspected lie are the chance to make short, accurate casts, and to keep most, if not all, of the line off the surface. The swirling currents, which are such valuable camouflage, cause serious drag problems, so the less line on the water, the better.

PAUL MARRINER

ooo **38** ooo

Perfect the Tuck Cast

Developed primarily for nymph fishing, the tuck cast works with dry flies as well. In pocket water, where the target zones are small and drag sets in so quickly, it helps to get the fly on, or below, the surface before the leader.

PAUL MARRINER

Head-Wind Casting

One of the most perplexing situations beginners face while fly-casting is a head wind, which is almost a daily occurrence on many streams and lakes. Having a sudden gust of wind blow your line, leader, and fly back in your face is frustrating at best and dangerous at worst. Many people simply stop fishing when a head wind blows. This is not necessary, for learning a simple casting technique can effectively combat all but the most fierce head winds.

The key to beating a head wind is to modify the standard casting stroke to produce a very high back cast and a very low front cast. This can be accomplished easily by paying attention to the rod position during the casting.

The head-wind cast works best casting the rod through the vertical plane, that is, perpendicular to the surface of the water, not dropping the rod toward the sidearm position. Bring the rod up quickly from the 9 o'clock position to *no further back* than the 12 o'clock position. Many times, stopping at the 11 o'clock position works well. A sudden stop at this position should have the effect of sending the back cast very high behind you. Watching the back cast and thinking about sending the back cast "straight up" will help. Then, after the standard pause to load the rod with the back cast, cast the rod forward to the 9 o'clock position, creating a very low front cast. When you are false-casting, the fly should nearly touch the water on the forward cast.

Holding your elbow higher than you normally would helps produce a casting stroke that is more "up and down" than "back and forth." Done properly, this cast effectively drives the line down toward your target rather than holding it up where the wind can wreak havoc with it. Practice it on a calm day, and then, when a head wind does blow, you can keep on fishing!

LYNDON LAMPERT

For those of us who have spent years fly-fishing, it seems as though we enjoy making our experience more and more challenging. Fishing small streams, with their normal abundance of riparian habitat, can be especially challenging. The flora can consume a massive amount of flies. So casting becomes the name of the game in these small-stream situations.

Being able to perform more casts than just a roll cast is of great benefit to the angler. When it is possible, controlled false-casting gives you the ability to shoot more line and have better line control. The idea, of course, is to position the line to maximize your ability to put the fly right where you want it. In tight places on small streams, the landing area may be the size of a plate.

When casting in these surroundings, I sometimes turn my body sideways to the casting stroke. For a right-handed caster, the left shoulder turns toward the direction of the forward cast, the right shoulder to the rear. This way you can watch your cast in both directions, usually (hopefully) keeping the line out of the trees and hitting closer to your target. Most times, one cast is all you will get.

LOREN BRADLEY

ooo **41** ooo

I have discovered as a fly-fishing guide that most of my clients come to me as novice casters. Many overestimate their ability to cast. They want to run the Boston Marathon before they can even run a mile, before they can even walk. Most can metaphorically only crawl, their casting skills are that rudimentary. This is the very best time to develop *bad* habits by rushing the development of their casting skills (or lack thereof). This is a good lesson for those of you who have taken lessons or are self-taught and whose trips to the river or lake are few and far between. It is easy to misjudge your casting talents; if you do not catch the mistakes in time, they will become ingrained in your mind and muscle memory.

Try to be patient. All of us had to start from the beginning at some point. Most of us were not casting like Lefty Kreh by the end of the third day on the water. In fact, only Lefty Kreh will ever cast as well as Lefty Kreh. Remember that casting perfectly is only a small part of what fly-fishing is really about. But the better you can cast, the more ammo you have at your disposal to catch more fish. But be honest with yourself about your skill level as well as with your guide or instructor.

I like to teach and emphasize only one casting skill at a time. I break the act of casting into as many small procedures as possible, baby steps if you will. A review of the basic tenets is always a good idea if your casting is rusty. Try it out in your backyard where your mistakes won't have an audience. Or better yet, try practicing with a friend. It is easier to alter bad habits with an extra set of eyes.

Begin by practicing your rod position (10 to 2 o'clock) with only the rod, no lines in the guides. The wrist shouldn't break, the elbow remains next to the ribs, and the thumb wraps around the cork handle.

Emphasize even timing between the casting strokes as well as equal energy pushing the rod forward and pulling it backward. Make sure the rod freezes in each position. Whether you are casting four feet or forty feet, these basics do not change.

Next, add one rod length of fly-line plus the leader (no fly just yet). Control the line by holding it next to the handle with the index finger of the casting hand (the right hand for a right-handed caster). The other hand (left hand) should relax. When you understand (or remember) how to fully extend the line forward and backward, change control of the fly-line to the left hand, then repeat the forward and backward motion (10 to 2 o'clock).

Next, practice false-casting four times and drop then point the rod tip where you want the fly to land. Make sure the fly-line straightens completely out on each casting stroke and when you drop the rod tip. If you encounter problems, go back sequentially in your practice strokes to find the steps you find difficult to execute.

Of course, all this is abbreviated and will be sequentially different for each person. We all learn at different rates, with varying amounts of practice. The most important thing to take away from practicing is to learn how to cast step by step. Make all the casting skills as simple as possible. Add each skill layer on layer. Don't add a new skill until you can master the previous skill. Patience and practice will determine whether or not you carry bad habits to the stream, habits hard to break. Always remember: (1) rod position 10 to 2 o'clock; (2) precise, even timing between casting strokes; (3) equal energy on backward cast (pulling) and the forward cast (pushing).

DOUG CAMP

∘∘∘ **42** ∘∘∘

Paint your splitshot with high-visibility jig paint. This allows you to track your nymph as it drifts downstream, sort of like an underwater "strike indicator." The fish rarely care, and many is the time we have had fish pick up the bright orange splitshot in preference to the fly.

RALPH AND LISA CUTTER

ooo **43** ooo

We always get a lot of interest from anglers peering over our shoulders because we glue our leaders to our fly-lines using Zap-a-Gap. This setup gives us a smooth transition between our fly-line and leader; the line will not hang up in the guides or catch in the weeds. When the splice is properly performed, the line is strong enough that it is never the weak link in our system. Joe Robinson of the Austin Angler taught us this trick years ago.

JEFF AND CYNDIE SCHMITT

ooo **44** ooo

We like to fish streamers from a boat and tend to lose a lot of streamers when we cast aggressively around cover. In order to minimize time tying on new streamers and risk missing good water, we prerig a handful of streamers before we go out. We use a perfection loop-to-loop rig to connect the tippet to the leader. We then rig a streamer with a Trilene knot to the hook and make a perfection loop about 12 inches up. We store these ready-to-use rigs on one of those spring-loaded plastic nelled-hook holders. When we break off, we just grab one, rig up and get to casting again.

JEFF AND CYNDIE SCHMITT

○○○ **45** ○○○

Here's a simple tip that will help you catch more fish: Grease the fly-line with silicone dressing. Since the current beneath the surface is faster than the surface, the tippet and line under the water cause drag and can sink the fly. Apply silicone dressing to get your line to ride high and you'll have less drag, more fish.

HARRY MURRAY

○○○ **46** ○○○

We are convinced that the best connection for the leader to your fly-line is a nail knot. Purchase a Tie-Fast knot tool (five bucks at your local fly-shop); it will be one of the best investments that you will ever make in fly-fishing. This tool allows you to tie painless nail knots in seconds. The best reason to use nail knots over braided loops is that they will pass easily through the guides of the rod. We have seen countless fish lost with a long leader and a braided loop (and the perfection or surgeon loop knot that connects the leader to the loop) hangs in the guides or the tip-top and the fish is broken off.

If you feel that you want to use loop-to-loop connections and you choke at the price of "premade loops," it is a simple procedure to make them yourself. Cortland sells braided mono running line that is designed as a running line for shooting heads. It comes in 30- and 50-pound test and 100-foot spools. We use 50-pound for all my saltwater lines (every saltwater line we own has a large braided loop attached to both ends, braided loops are great for saltwater fly-fishing, but that's another subject). For all freshwater applications you would want to use 30-pound test.

Cut off a 6-inch section of the braided

mono. Take a 12-inch section of fine wire (size # 3 single-strand fishing wire works best) and bend it in half with pliers. This is your threading tool. Insert the tool into the braided mono and thread it through the hollow middle of the mono for about one inch.

Push the tool out of the side of the braided mono and insert the tag end of the mono into the "eye" of your tool. Pull the end of the mono back through the center of the braided mono and out the side where the tool was inserted. Continue pulling until the desired loop size is achieved, 1 inch or less. Cut the mono about 1 inch (3 inches for saltwater) behind the loop. Thread your fly-line into the hollow core of the braided mono.

A drop of superglue will attach it permanently to your line, or you can take your Tie Fast tool and tie a nail knot (3 knots for saltwater) on top of the braided mono, cinching it to your fly-line. A spool of Cortland braided mono should make 200-plus loops at a cost of pennies each. We hope that this helps to answer your question. Good fishing!

TERRY GUNN AND WENDY HANVOLD-GUNN

∘∘∘ **47** ∘∘∘

Whether you are a beginner or an expert, your knots can't be too good. And you're bound to be a bit rusty early in the season, so practice your preferred knots when the snow flies. Are they neat? Do they seat properly? Can you tie them with consistency? There's a certain Zen quality to the satisfaction brought by a well-tied knot—not to mention the satisfaction of losing fewer fish.

JIM BUTLER

∘∘∘ **48** ∘∘∘

Ball-and-Chain Nymphing Rig

The traditional method of weighting leaders for nymph fishing is to add small split-shot or twisted lead strips to the leader 10 to 18 inches above the nymph. This method works fine, but the "ball-and-chain" system works even better. Instead of adding weight to the leader, tie an additional piece of tippet 7 to 9 inches long to the eye of the nymph with a standard clinch knot. This is the "chain." Tie a simple overhand knot near the free end of the chain. Place splitshot above the knot. This is the "ball."

The ball-and-chain method has two advantages over the traditional weighting method. First, if the lead hangs up with the traditional rig, you'll likely lose both your weight and your nymph. When you hang bottom with the ball-and-chain method, you'll usually lose just the weight, especially if you use a chain of equal or smaller diameter than the tippet of your leader.

The second advantage of this system is increased sensitivity to the take. Unlike the traditional method, there is nothing between the fish and your strike indicator to impede the pause or twitch of the indicator. The increased number of hookups is well worth the small amount of extra effort to rig the ball and chain.

LYNDON LAMPERT

∘∘∘ **49** ∘∘∘

Double-Rigged Flies

It has been my experience over many years of fishing and guiding that fishing two flies, particularly when nymphing, can increase the frequency of strikes manyfold. A two-fly setup consists of a top fly (either a dry or a nymph) and a dropper fly (usually a smaller fly, usually a nymph) attached to the top fly with a 12 to 18 inch piece of tippet. The greatest difficulty in fishing with two flies is the tendency for your gear to tangle.

To set up a tangle-free rig, attach the tippet of the dropper fly to the bend of the upper hook of the top fly. I like to use an improved clinch knot to attach the dropper tippet to the hook of the top fly. The bump of the barb and the direction the fish pulls prevent the tippet from slipping off. The in-line sequence of this rig seldom tangles.

The dropper rig can be especially productive when you combine an attractor fly pattern (the top fly) with an emerger or nymph (the dropper fly). The presence of the attractor fly will often accomplish the first goal of of the dropper rig, that of causing the fish to look toward your flies. The fish may then notice your trailing fly, the dropper fly, which it might not otherwise see. This recognition often triggers the fish to strike at one of the two flies, usually but not always to smaller dropper fly.

Another advantage of a dropper rig is that the larger fly tends to act as a gentle weight and holds the dropper fly near the bottom of the water where the fish most often hold and feed. Keep the dropper tippet between the two flies relatively short, 8 to 16 inches. This prevents the dropper fly from floating up out of the zone. The delicate weight of the upper fly also facilitates a more natural float of the lower fly.

I also use a lighter-weight tippet to connect the top fly to the dropper fly. This allows more flexibility in the short tippet. It breaks off first and prevents the loss of both flies if the lower fly is hung up.

When attaching weight to the tippet, whether splitshot or twist-ons, place it above the top fly, never between the two flies. The weight should usually be located quite close to the top fly, about 8 inches up, to keep the two flies ticking along the bottom in the holding layer.

Barrie Bush

ooo **50** ooo

One of the most important elements of fly-fishing is the presentation of your fly to the fish. When fishing for salmon and steelhead, I have found time and time again that if you can get your fly close to the fish and properly present the pattern, you will have a better chance of hooking them. You will need to keep your rod tip low and follow your line as it drifts along. For salmon and steelhead, this often means getting the fly down to where the fish are holding, meaning you will need to use sinking lines.

The tip section of the sinking lines sinks very fast, putting the fly at the correct depth for a longer period of time. I recommend the Teeny T-Series of sinking lines with a short leader of 3 to 4 feet. Many anglers who fish with a sinking line use too long a leader. The short leader gets the fly down quickly, puts it down with the line, and keeps it down longer.

The speed of the current and depth of the water (as well as your rod size) will determine which weight of sinking line you should fish with. The T-Series comes in different grain weights ranging from 130 to 500 grains. The heavier the grains, the heavier the line and the faster it will sink. The bigger-sized lines require heavier-weight rods accordingly.

JIM TEENY

∘∘∘ **51** ∘∘∘

During a major caddis hatch, it is important to mimic the flight of the caddis as closely as possible. When caddis are hopping all over the surface, forget casting if the trout are rising all around you. Instead, hold your rod up high and bounce an Elk Hair Caddis or other imitation off the surface to imitate the erratic movement of the ongoing hatch. The thrill of shortlining a close-by slashing trout is hard to beat for thrills.

BOB NEWMAN

°°° **52** °°°

When browns, brookies, and other trout turn off standard dry flies, try a terrestrial like a Joe's Hopper. A radical change-up like this is often all a stuffed trout needs to wake up and smell the chow. The sudden appearance of a fat hopper overhead seems to break the trout's complacency after it has dined heavily on aquatic insects like mayflies and caddis.

BOB NEWMAN

°°° **53** °°°

Tie bivisible posts on your parachute dry-fly patterns. A tuft of white and another

tuft of black calf body fur laid against one
another make a post that is visible both in
shadows and glare.

RALPH AND LISA CUTTER

∘∘∘ **54** ∘∘∘

It took me years to realize that largemouth bass gather in the shallows after
dragonflies. They'll charge them when
they flounder on the water and even leap
to snatch them from a reed. When largemouths want dragonflies, they'll often
settle for nothing else.

There are good flies for imitating dragons. The Betts' Foam Dragon, David
Lucca's Foam Dragonfly, and the Whitlock's Krystal Dragon are all well estab-
lished and well proven.

Put a dragon right next to cover, usually in the shallows; work it a little, just a
twitch or shudder now and then, though
once in a while a lively panicked action is
best. And keep your wits—largemouths
take dragons with violence!

SKIP MORRIS

ooo **55** ooo

When you tie or buy flies for the hatches you fish, think in terms of pattern styles that match the different insect orders. Then tie size and color variations of the styles for the species within each order. Species in all of the aquatic insect orders vary in size and color, but not in shape.

DAVE HUGHES

ooo **56** ooo

Carry a small range of dry flies, wets, nymphs, and streamers to cover the narrow color and size range of the most common natural food forms in their most common shapes. Three to four dozen carefully selected flies in olive, sulfur, gray, and black will let you match hatches anywhere.

DAVE HUGHES

∘∘∘ **57** ∘∘∘

Use Large Dry Flies

Fish holding in pockets have but an instant to make a take-or-refuse decision. Occasionally, hatch matching may be necessary, but more often a large attractor fly is best. Flies in sizes 10 to 14 offer an attractive morsel and stand up better to the rapid casting required.

PAUL MARRINER

∘∘∘ **58** ∘∘∘

Keep the Stone-Fly Box Handy

On streams with pocket water, I invariably switch to a large stone-fly nymph if dry flies don't work. Pocket water is natural stone-fly habitat and the trout there are accustomed to seeing big stone-fly nymphs. Such imitations can be heavily weighted to reach the taking zone quickly with a tuck cast. Even if the big flies don't work, I will usually switch to a smaller stone-fly pattern rather than a mayfly nymph or caddis worm. Even in pocket

water too warm for stone flies, I have
found that smallmouth bass have a taste
for them.

PAUL MARRINER

ᴏᴏᴏ **59** ᴏᴏᴏ

Most tips are old tricks. Here's a good
one to use when you are fishing dry flies.
If you are fishing a conventional dry fly
and getting plenty of looks or short
strikes, try trimming the hackle off the
bottom of the fly. This makes the fly float
flush on the surface. Once the fly more
closely imitates the natural insect's float,
you'll see a higher percentage of hookups.

In fact, always carry a small pair of
scissors and you can modify your dry flies
for current conditions. A dry fly can become an emerger or a crippled dun, even
a nymph, something the fish may be key-
ing on. And this with just a simple snip
or two.

STEPHEN TRAMMEL

∘∘∘ **60** ∘∘∘

As a beginning fly-fisherman devouring angling books the way a brown trout does stone flies, I was captivated by the concept of matching the hatch. Its elegant simplicity—find out what the fish are eating and fool them with a mimic clump of feathers and fur—appealed to my basic nature as an intertwining of science and art.

After I'd put in more hours on the water than in the armchair, however, I discovered that hatch matching isn't the all-encompassing answer that I was led to believe, particularly on my home waters in the southern Rockies. As these streams tumble out of the mountains, they take great leaps from boulder to boulder, creating a mosaic of foam, chop, and glare. Far too often my drab, realistic pattern gets lost in the complexity of the currents, or worse, my attention is called to an unseen fly by the flash of a trout I've just missed.

Since high-country trout are notably unfussy, you can increase your chance of success in water flowing swiftly over rocks by using a pattern that is suitable for the character of the stream regardless of what naturals are on the surface. Simply put, you need to match the water, not the hatch, and high-floating, high-visibility patterns are the key.

For the riffles and choppy currents typical of freestone streams, select a high-floating pattern. Heavy-hackled, hair-winged flies like the Wulff series were designed with just such water in mind. Hair-bodied flies—the redoubtable Humpy, Irresistible, and Goddard Caddis—also ride high in the currents and can take repeated dunkings and remain afloat. If you desire a more realistic silhouette, try slender-bodied fore-and-aft patterns like the Renegade.

For the cascading currents found in pocket water, use a good floater with light-colored, high-profile wings. Upright white wings are often best in low-light situations and patterns like the Royal Humpy or parachute versions of common flies are ideal choices. At midday, light elk hair or golden poly yarn wings make the fly stand out against the white background of foam. When fishing dry flies, you rarely catch fish if you don't see the strike. Besides, the fundamental excitement of fly-fishing a mountain stream stems from watching the quick grab from a once-hidden trout.

CRAIG MARTIN

∘∘∘ **61** ∘∘∘

The adult smallmouth bass is piscivorous (as well as inquisitive) and eats minnows, crayfish, and other forage fish. These fish like big groceries. So take advantage of the smallmouth's curiosity and throw some big and gaudy flies at them. Most of the time, you will want to fish underwater for the smallmouth and the most successful patterns for subsurface fishing include woolly buggers (in olive, black, or brown), crayfish patterns, and the reliable Clouser Minnow (especially a white and chartreuse pattern).

The key to fishing with streamers is to get the fly to the bottom quickly, get control of your line and leader, be in direct contact with your fly as it bumps along the bottom, and have a drag-free presentation. A faster-action rod will keep you in closer contact with your fly, allowing you more hookups.

Smallmouth bass will also smash to smithereens a big, juicy top-water popper. Top-water fishing for bronzebacks is one of the most exciting way to fly-fish. The bass slash to the top early in the morning and late in the evening, even in clear water. On cloudy water or on overcast days, you can sometimes catch fish all day long with top-water patterns.

TOM THEUS

∘∘∘ **62** ∘∘∘

Caddisflies

A knowledge of basic caddis habits is essential for success during much of the season. It is largely caddis emergences that baffle fishermen, and merely being able to recognize when caddis are hatching is the critical first step in understanding caddis.

In his book *Caddisflies,* Gary LaFontaine notes three signs that indicate when caddis are emerging on rivers, and they are worth repeating. First, trout occasionally are seen leaping in the air. He notes this happens when trout chase emerging caddis pupae; the fish's momentum sometimes carries it right out of the water.

The second clue is that there are no insects on the water. Even during a heavy emergence, adult caddis are just about impossible to see drifting on the surface. They generally emerge and fly off unnoticed. This phenomenon always amazes us. Many times we have held our noses at water level just below a pocket full of trout rising madly to caddis, to see just one adult fly off. Indeed, it is nothing short of a miracle if you do.

Third, LaFontaine writes that most of the feeding trout are bulging and splashing. This occurs as the fish take the pupae from the surface film and turn downward. While this is sometimes true, we find that the rise form is more dependent on the speed of the current the fish is in rather than the food being taken. That is, in fast water bulging and splashing does occur, but in slower water, quiet dimples, porpoise rolls, or tails breaking the surface are much more common rise forms. It is important to consider the rise form in deciding what a trout may be taking, but it is wise never to make a judgment based solely on it.

We think that the strongest clue to a caddis hatch, aside from knowing what insects to expect is that no insects are seen on the water, and yet fish are rising.

CRAIG MATHEWS AND JOHN JURACEK

∘∘∘ **63** ∘∘∘

Keep your prime dry-fly and nymphing rods strung and stored in one of the new covered PVC rod-and-reel tubes. Then you can grab the tube and your loaded duffle and you'll never forget a thing you need for a short trip. You'll also be rigged and fishing faster when you get to the water.

DAVE HUGHES

∘∘∘ **64** ∘∘∘

Keep your essential fly-fishing gear—
waders, brogues, reels, fly boxes, vest,
rain jacket, hat, gloves, long johns, etc.—
stored in a wader duffle that is always
packed, ready to grab and go. You can
rush out the door to go fishing with the
assurance that you won't be forgetting
anything.

DAVE HUGHES

∘∘∘ **65** ∘∘∘

You may not realize just how much
money (or sentimentality) you've got tied
up in your fly-fishing gear. I learned the
hard way a few years back when a sub-
stantial amount of my fly-fishing life was
"redirected" as checked baggage on an
airline flight. The things I learned as I
went through a frantic and unsuccessful
attempt to recover my lost gear may help
you a bit.

If you are like me, it is very tempting to
be organized. I had purchased one of
those "put everything in me" combination
rod cases/gear bags. I stashed nearly

everything but my waders in there. The bag looked nice and made me feel the part of the "Joe Fly-Fisherman" since it had everything but the words "Take Me" stenciled on the side. The combination bag was too obvious fishing gear, no doubt a package deal at the local pawn-shop the next morning.

My advice is to pack things separately in more regular-looking bags, bags without small, accessible pockets on the side so that mischievous hands cannot easily check the contents. Carry what you can on the plane with you, and make those things the most valuable of your gear, the gear you could least do without. And these things are not always your most expensive gear either.

Read the small print on your airline ticket. You might be amazed at what is *not* covered as lost baggage. Many valuable things are not covered. And even though reimbursement limits for lost items have increased the last few years, the amounts are likely well below the replacement cost of your equipment. Check your homeowner's policy to see what coverage may be afforded there—

it's a lot cheaper to add protection that way than it is to buy the additional coverage from the airline on a trip-by-trip basis.

I prefer to use my two-piece fly-rods even though they do take up some space in their tubes. I used to check them but since my incident, I carry them with me at all times. Two rods in bags will generally fit into one aluminum rod tube. I carry a handy tube, bigger than most, which holds four rods plus my wading staff. I use it like a cane and will *not* check it at the ticket counter. The tube usually fits in the overhead compartment or in the closet. In the event the tube does not fit in either, I demand that the rod tube be "gate checked."

You may request that the airline take small bags from you at the door of the plane, provide you with a claim check, run it by hand down those little stairs on the concourse, and return it to you at the arrival gate, not at baggage claim.

In short, with regard to checked baggage, don't take it for granted that your valuable possessions are in good hands with the personnel behind the counter wall. I have heard horror stories from many others about the loss, destruction, or theft of their fly-fishing gear. In fact, the more valuable your bags are, or the more valuable they look, the more I would worry. Furthermore, don't believe you can or will necessarily get justice if something is lost.

I recommend that you keep all your important gear with you, and if you cannot do that, at least have a backup reel with line and other important goodies in a separate bag. A loaded reel and fly-box fit easily in a carry-on bag.

After getting over the hassle and trauma of losing all of my equipment, I set about replacing it and in doing so, I came across Hexagraph fly-rods. One thing led to another and I eventually bought the company. So even bad things often have good consequences. But I still wish I had the box of 1960s stone flies back.

HARRY BRISCOE

ooo **66** ooo

Clean Your Fly-Line. Why? Because I Said So!

Imagine that you have just arrived at your favorite fishing spot. It is a beautiful day and the conditions are drop-dead perfect. A monster hatch of *callibaetis* is beginning to cover the water and the fish look like they are playing a game of water polo under the belly boat.

Suddenly, the wind kicks up, the hatch ends and the fish move to beyond your normal casting range. Now what do you do? Well, why don't you try cleaning your fly-line while you have some spare time? Cleaning your fly-line is a guaranteed way to improve casting distance immediately. No practice or classes necessary.

Have you ever been in your "zone" casting hard and fast only to hear the sound of coarse-grade sandpaper rubbing on a mystery object? That is the sound of dirt and sand on your fly-line rubbing tiny grooves in the ferrules of your fly-rod. If you don't want your rod ferrules to wear down to the nubbins, you owe it to yourself to double the life of your line and your rod by taking a few minutes to clean the line.

Another reason to clean the line is that with a dirty line, your nymphing will suffer, since the fly-line sinks faster than your fly. If you remove the excess dirt, film, and scum, your line will float higher and float longer. A clean line also makes mending easier, since the drag is reduced.

It is easy to clean the fly-line. Take a clean cotton ball and lay the tag end of the fly-line in the middle of the cotton ball. Wrap the cotton ball around the fly-line and squeeze it tight with your thumb and fingers.

Now strip the line through the cotton ball down to the backing. Take a look at the cotton ball and be amazed at the dirt. Wind the fly-line back in and repeat the process, only this time, grab another cotton ball and add a short spray of Armor All to the ball. You can also use products like Glide or 3M's mastery line cleaner. There are also various other cleaning pads available at fly-shops to use in place of the cotton ball, but the cotton balls are cheaper and work well.

Whatever you do, remember to add this quick and simple maintenance to your pretrip repertoire and your line will last longer, your mends will be sharper and casts will be longer.

Doug Camp

∘∘∘ **67** ∘∘∘

An early lesson I learned was always to lubricate my fly-reel. We all forget or are too lazy to take the thirty seconds to perform such a menial chore, but by periodically lubricating your reels, you will add both performance and longevity to them. Check your owner's manual for more specific instructions. Beware that many disc drag reels do not need oiling. I always use Loon Reel Lube, especially since it is biodegradable, but there are many other dependable lubricants on the market.

Marcos Enriquez

Reading the Water

∘∘∘ **68** ∘∘∘

Survey the area you are fishing, note
where the rocks lie, where the crosscurrents run. Angle upstream and to the side
at a 45-degree angle to get better drag
control. Then cast slightly upstream. This
simple act allows the angler to better control the line.

HARRY MURRAY

∘∘∘ **69** ∘∘∘

Cast across grass beds where the fish can
find refuge. The water in these areas is
usually low and clear, so be sure to hide
your approach.

HARRY MURRAY

∘∘∘ **70** ∘∘∘

In flowing water, smallmouth are going to be where the most amount of food goes by and where the least effort is required to remain. Structure and habitat are two often-used words among veteran anglers. They are topics that should be in the minds of all anglers when approaching a body of water.

Most spots in a river with fast-moving current lanes near slow-water areas will hold fish. River fish take up residence in holding spots near flowing food lanes. They wait on the current's edge for food to be carried down to them—very much the way you would while walking down a cafeteria line.

MARK KOVACH

∘∘∘ **71** ∘∘∘

Fish-riffled currents and pockets—fish find these easy holding spots. Don't bypass the current slicks—they often hold big fish. Fish all the slack water, especially in front or behind structures.

MARK KOVACH

∘∘∘ **72** ∘∘∘

Learn to recognize empty water and don't waste time fishing it. If you can save the time spent fishing empty water, and shift it to fishing likely lies, you'll quickly become one of the 10 percent of the fishermen rumored to catch 90 percent of the trout, because you'll be where the trout hang out.

DAVE HUGHES

∘∘∘ **73** ∘∘∘

Work All the Hot Spots

Remember that trout hold in the hydraulic cushion in front of and beside rocks as well as on the inside of those attractive seams behind the rock.

PAUL MARRINER

∘∘∘ **74** ∘∘∘

A good pair of lightweight binoculars can not only entertain you with beautiful vistas but can help spot subtle rises and other fishy activity. From a driftboat, you can see bank risers that are active in the shadows in only inches of water. Use the glasses to spot birds, too. Swallows in active, swooping dives will indicate hatching insects and, usually, busy fish.

Also, use binoculars to scan side channels for risers and other activity. The glasses come in handy for observing other fishermen who are having success when you are experiencing a notable lack. And finally, binoculars provide a close-up but discreet view of female swimsuit beauties on hot Montana days.

STEPHEN TRAMMEL

∘∘∘ **75** ∘∘∘

Northern pike and other dominant fish predators in rivers always take the best ambush lies. Usually, they will be where the food fish of choice congregrate and must pass during spawning, migration, or daily ritual. In rivers such as the Rio Grande in New Mexico, a choice spot for a lie is where a rivulet or small stream runs into the river, bringing the sand out into the channel.

There you will usually find an eddy, with a bankside upstream. At these junctions, you will also usually find a dropoff channel at the end of the current flow. The predator waits at this dropoff.

From the eddy-side, upstream bank, cast across the eddy into the main current letting the floating line be swept upstream by the countercurrent. A large weighted streamer will automatically be pulled slowly upstream along this dropoff edge, emulating a small dumb fish looking for food in the current seam. Be sure to use a very sharp hook with a depressed barb, since the predator fish must hook itself on the take.

JERRAL DERRYBERRY

°°° **76** °°°

The smallmouth bass is the perfect fish. It is aggressive, acrobatic, beautiful, readily available, and a great fighter. To be a successful smallmouth bass fly-rodder, you must know how to read the water. Look for water that has medium visibility, since clear water will make the fish spooky and they will feed mostly at night. In cloudy water, the bass will have difficulty in seeing your fly.

Your three most important clues to reading the water and finding where the bronzebacks are located are: safety, shelter, and food. Look for the deeper pools, rocks, rockbeds, obstructions, outside bends, and undercuts. The bigger fish will hold in the prime lies.

Work the water thoroughly and slowly. Use your stalking skills to help you catch more fish. Make your presentations not only in front of the boulder, but to the middle, to the edges, and behind the boulder. Cover the entire area.

TOM THEUS

∘∘∘ **77** ∘∘∘

The larger fish in a small stream tend to inhabit the undercut banks, overhanging areas and the all-around tougher places to fish. The big fish has only three basic concerns in life: eat, not be eaten (or caught and released), and make little replicas of themselves. Generally, other than in spawning season, small stream fish are elusive and wary of predators. As we wade the streams, we need to keep in mind that fish will be sensitive to movement in and around the water. The majority of the time it is difficult to stay out of the stream, given the thick tree-lined banks, so care must be taken to disturb the stream as little as possible.

LOREN BRADLEY

∘∘∘ **78** ∘∘∘

One of the things I have discovered when fishing for trout on streams is that many trout hold in shallow lies less than a foot wide, often tucked away under a limb or tight between two rocks. Most anglers like the easy way out, preferring to cast to wide, open lies instead of cover around overhanging limbs and other obstacles.

If you aren't casting to the places where it's hard to get a drift, then you're missing out on a lot of trout. Cast close to the banks, up against the rocks, to water as shallow as your ankles, to water as small as a teacup. You'll be rewarded many times over.

ED ADAMS

∘∘∘ **79** ∘∘∘

The next time you are fishing for land-lock salmon and they get finicky, try nymphs, wets, and dry flies imitating caddis and mayflies. Studies show that landlocks dine much more heavily on aquatic insects in all stages of their lives than most anglers believe.

Landlocked salmon are one of Maine's most beloved game fish, and anglers from far and away seek them with streamer flies such as the classic Gray Ghost, Nine-Three, Warden's Worry, Queen Bee, and Kennebago Smelt. But sometimes, landlocks in rivers and streams decide they don't want anything imitating a smelt or baitfish; they want insects.

BOB NEWMAN

∘∘∘ **80** ∘∘∘

Fly-Fishing for Chums and Silvers

The biggest runs of chum and silver salmon occur in Alaska. When they begin their spawning migration, they usually enter fresh water en masse. Although they have stopped feeding they still possess an instinctive competitiveness. For several years they have survived and grown in the ocean by chasing their prey. That competitiveness stays with them in fresh water.

Silvers and chums often make their presence know by rolling or creating V-wakes as they swim upstream. When I see the location of fish I try to lead the fish, dropping my fly 10 to 15 feet above it. I begin to strip the fly just after it hits the water. On large rivers, like the Nushagak or Alagnak, V-wakes appear as fish follow the fly. On smaller, clear streams the fish may be visible. As the fish close on the fly I accelerate the strip speed. This nearly always results in a solid take.

Two excellent flies for silvers and chums are the Pink Polly Wog and Orange

Admiral. The Polly Wog is a surface fly. Fish it with a floating line. The Orange Admiral is a wet fly and can be fished on either floating or sinking line.

Pink Polly Wog

Hook: long shank size 2–⅙.
Tail: pink marabou with a few strands of pink or silver Flashabou.
Body: pink deer hair clipped to a fairly flat disk shape.

Orange Admiral

Hook: any standard salmon or 1xL streamer hook size 6-1.
Tail: orange marabou with 4–6 strands of silver Flashabou.
Body: either orange chenille with silver tinsel in it or orange Cactus chenille.
Wing: orange marabou with 4–6 strands of Flashabou.
Eyes: silver bead chain or chrome dumbbell (optional).

Marty Sherman

∘∘∘ **81** ∘∘∘

Drift boats are designed with casting stations in the front and back of the boat. These stations are essentially upright yokes that surround the standing angler's hips. The casting stations are facing downstream for a reason. You are traveling downstream and that's where all the targets will be found. Sounds simple, but you'd be surprised how many anglers make locating targets and casting to those targets more difficult than need be. Try to remember to stand centered in the casting stations, anticipate where you want to make your next cast, and you'll always be ready for upcoming casting targets.

TIM LINEHAN

∘∘∘ **82** ∘∘∘

When float-fishing, don't get sidetracked by action behind you. Don't worry if a five-pound rainbow just snapped a grasshopper off the surface, because you'll be floating several miles during the day and will have ample opportunities at other big fish. If you turn around and cast upstream, your fly is likely to drag and your success will be limited. Instead, concentrate on downstream targets, on accurate casting and mending, and keeping your fly on the water drag-free for as long as possible. With this premise in mind, you'll find yourself hooking more fish.

TIM LINEHAN

∘∘∘ **83** ∘∘∘

Fly-fishing in lakes or stillwaters often means getting a fly down to the depth at which the fish are actually feeding. Once there, it is important to maintain and retrieve the fly through that feeding zone for as much of the cast as possible. Fishing from an anchored boat or other floating device gives the angler much greater control over the retrieve and also detection of strikes. When you are fishing out of a boat the use of only one anchor can be a very frustrating experience.

Changing wind direction will swing a boat back and forth or, in the worst scenario, continually turn the craft in circles. Any thoughts of line control are quickly lost in this situation. Anchoring the boat at the bow and stern will keep it from shifting in the wind and give that needed line control to detect even the slightest strikes.

Double anchoring is particularly important when fishing midge or chironomid hatches. Midge pupa do not swim to the surface of the lake but rise vertically through the water column. Pupal imitations must be retrieved very slowly or "dead drifted" to be effective. Any sudden movement of the pupal pattern will affect the way it is presented to the trout and thus impact on your fishing success.

BRIAN CHAN

∘∘∘ **84** ∘∘∘

Drift Boat Tips

Every year I can count on seeing a recurring scene; a vehicle stuck at a boat launch or takeout. This usually occurs because the driver feels he must back his trailer completely into the river to unload or load the boat. This is not the case. Drift boats are quite light and easy to slide across land ground or pavement. The only thing that immersing the trailer accomplishes is to ruin the wheel bearings.

A lining rope of 50 to 80 feet is often very useful to carry in your boat. Western rivers can easily change channels over the course of a year. High water sometimes undercuts banks, causing trees to fall across a channel. A lining rope attached to the bow will often allow you to pass your boat through an area where you may not be able to row. I've also found a use for my lining rope at rough takeouts where I can't get my trailer close to the boat. I simply attach the rope and slowly pull the boat to a point where the trailer is accessible.

MARTY SHERMAN

∘∘∘ **85** ∘∘∘

Survival Pack

For the angler who is visiting a wilderness fly-out lodge I advise carrying a basic survival kit. In fifteen years of experience fishing some fine Alaska fly-out lodges I only twice saw a guide pack any survival gear. While it is true I have never been stranded overnight during any fly-out fishing, it doesn't hurt to be prepared. It could prevent a very uncomfortable experience. These are also good items to carry for anglers doing day hikes into remote streams.

List:

emergency survival bag (this weighs only ounces)

fire-starter kit

*high-energy, lightweight food: dry fruit,
    jerky, hard candy*

small flashlight

MARTY SHERMAN

∘∘∘ **86** ∘∘∘

Wade with Common Sense

Wading close is often an advantage in catching fish, but no fish is worth dying for. Heavy pocket water can be dangerous. Always carry a wading staff and place your feet carefully—it's easy to trip or twist an ankle among the stones. Wading is a skill that is rarely taught and novices can learn a great deal from an experienced wader. Even after thirty years of practice, I prefer to have a buddy in the vicinity. Finally, never wade into uncomfortable water, since it can be damn difficult to get back if the current or depth become unmanageable.

PAUL MARRINER

○○○ **87** ○○○

Landing fish you intend to release can sometimes be harmful to the fish if you attempt to do it from a boat. Generally you must remove the fish from the water to free the hook. This deprives the fish of oxygen it can get only by being submerged in the water. It also provides an opportunity to be dropped in the boat. If possible, when releasing fish beach the boat and get out so you can keep the fish in the water. If beaching is impossible, at least keep the fish over the water while handling.

MARTY SHERMAN

∘∘∘ **88** ∘∘∘

Though sinking lines are certainly the norm for fishing trout lakes because the trout are usually too deep for the surface fly, it surprises many anglers that a floating line can reach down, too. In British Columbia, Canada, the imitation chironomid pupa on a floating line and very long leader (up to 25 feet!) is common practice for fishing lakes. There, the method has been honed for decades—and it's deadly. The angler waits a long time for the lightly weighted fly to fully sink, then works it in sporadically and ever so slowly.

I've fished a well-weighted imitation mayfly nymph this same way with great success, though a bit more quickly. Any time the slow, deep fly is called for in a

lake, and the depth is not beyond, say, 25
feet, the floating line and long leader may
be the best solution.

SKIP MORRIS

000 **89** 000

It is pretty safe to say that catching trout
on dry flies is as good as it gets. Unfortunately, the majority of the feeding done
by trout in streams and lakes is subsurface. Feeding in deeper water not only
provides better protection from avian
predators (ospreys, eagles, herons) but
also requires less energy on the part of
the trout as migrating insect pupa and
nymphs are easier to pick off as they
migrate en mass to hatch.

One of the most versatile fly-lines for
fishing lakes or stillwaters is the intermediate or slow sinking line. These lines are
designed to sink at a very slow rate (generally between 1.25 and 1.75 inches/sec-
ond) which make them very effective for
fishing water less than 20 feet deep. The
majority of aquatic insects that trout feed
on live in the shallower areas of the lake

where plant life is abundant as a result of sunlight penetration and photosynthesis.

The very slow sinking nature of the intermediate fly-line allows the angler to retrieve imitations of midges, mayflies, damselflies, caddisflies and dragonflies very slowly through the water without getting caught up in the bottom vegetation. It is important for the angler to have the patience to wait for the fly-line to sink to the desired depth before beginning the proper retrieve for the insect being imitated.

BRIAN CHAN

∘∘∘ **90** ∘∘∘

The longer you keep the lure in the bass strike zone, the greater chance of drawing a strike. If you have been an out-and-out consumer of bass-fishing articles for very long, you have heard this axiom many times. Unfortunately, it is one of many generalities associated with bass fishing that doesn't necessarily always hold true. During some of the toughest angling situations, the opposite is true.

Three specific situations come to mind where moving a fly quickly through the strike zone works best. First, when fishing bass waters which have extremely good visibility, anglers will find that a popper or streamer quickly retrieved will draw bass from a great distance. Western bass anglers have known for years that spotted bass and smallmouth bass will charge a surface lure, when it is worked relatively fast, from depths of 20 feet or more.

In fact, any time fly anglers are targeting sight-oriented feeders such as smallmouth bass, retrieving a large fly quickly through the strike zone will draw vicious strikes. This is often true with trophy-size river smallmouth bass that normally will not readily hit an artificial lure. This spirited retrieve plays on the bass's need to strike quickly before opportunity passes out of range.

Finally, during severe frontal activity, when largemouth bass are normally reluctant to feed or strike out of aggression, anglers must rely on drawing out instinctive strikes. A fly moved quickly in and out of the strike zone often draws a strike when nothing else will. The fish has no choice; instinctively it must strike. Professional tournament anglers have proven this retrieve technique to be effective during tough post-front conditions.

PAUL A. CANADA

∘∘∘ **91** ∘∘∘

If you have ever fished stock ponds you have probably had your fly-line entangled with the ubiquitous shoreline vegetation, usually scrappy bushes determined to reach out and grab your line. I dislike using a stripping basket almost as much as I dislike untangling my line from the brush, so I carry a cheap mosquito net with me whenever I visit stock ponds.

You can buy mosquito netting for a couple of bucks from any army/navy surplus store. Cut it into a 3-foot-square piece, fold it up, shove it in your vest pocket and you can pull it out to toss over the thorny problem any time you want. This cover keeps the line from entangling in the branches when stripping, helps keep it straight, and allows you to more

fully cover a section of water without all
the frustration.

CRAIG KAUTSCH

∘∘∘ **92** ∘∘∘

A few years ago my son, Karl, described
the summit of Devils Tower in Wyoming.
He said it was flat on top with lots of
grass. I asked if there were any lakes to
fish and he said no. I then asked, "Then
why go there?"

Fishing is my primary purpose of
backpacking to remote areas. Every un-
needed ounce feels like a ton after hiking
three or four miles. Carrying everything
on my back gave me an incentive to cut
every unnecessary ounce. My backcoun-

try fly-fishing gear is now down to just over one pound.

The first essential item is a four-piece fly-rod. My pack has external side pockets, which holds the rod in its bag. I leave the case at home. Even though the rod is outside the pack, it's still protected since it's shorter than my pack. Weight is about four ounces. My reel is a single-action Orvis Battenkill.

With backing and fly-line, it comes to perhaps eight ounces. The greatest weight savings comes by eliminating two very heavy (relatively speaking) items—a vest and waders. I use the smallest model Wood River bag to store all of my gear except the rod. Because many backcountry high lakes are too cold to wade, I get along without waders. I do wear Gore-Tex™ boots, so by watching my step I can even find a way across most streams without getting too wet. Into my bag goes my reel, a single fly-box, spare leaders, tippet material, a knot tying tool, moldable weight, strike indicators, forceps, and fly floatant. Total weight of my fishing gear comes to about twenty ounces.

Why only one fly-box? To save bulk as well as weight. Even a small box will hold all the flies needed for a week of fishing. With the exception of a few Woolly Buggers, I take an assortment of small flies. Essential patterns include the Elk Hair Caddis, Humpy, Adams, Griffith Gnat, Orange Asher, Gold-ribbed Hare's Ear, Beadhead Caddis nymph, Scud, Egg, San Juan Worm, Ant, and Hopper. These patterns in an assortment of sizes will be adequate for almost all conditions.

On those occasions that I know will require waders, I take lightweights that run about twelve ounces, a pair of old wool socks, and tennis shoes or sandals. Even with this addition, my gear doesn't exceed four pounds. By packing smart, I have everything I need without requiring a visit to a masseuse when I get home.

AL MARLOWE

∘∘∘ **93** ∘∘∘

I see a number of inexperienced backcountry anglers every summer trudging up the trail into the upper meadows of

Slough Creek in Yellowstone National Park sporting their chest-high, neoprene waders in 80-degree weather. These same folks often have nothing else in hand but a fly-rod and a vest, and they are a long way from wading in the cooling river.

This is a terrible mistake many anglers make. Neoprene waders are naturally warm and do not breathe. Combine this with warm weather and physical activity, and they risk dehydration, heat sickness, or even heat stroke. Not to mention that hiking in neoprene waders is just plain uncomfortable.

Also, not only does hiking in felt-soled wading boots wear them out quickly, but the felt provides little traction on gravel trails. In short, to make the hike easier and safer, pack your waders, whether neoprene, canvas, nylon or hip waders in a backpack or daypack—don't wear them hiking.

CHAD OLSEN

∘∘∘ **94** ∘∘∘

One point I would like to get across to everyone traveling in the backcountry is to carry plenty of drinkable water. Water can mean the difference between life and death. Dehydration can lead to pulled muscles, fatigue, heat sickness, and heat stroke.

Symptoms include dark urine, headaches, dizziness, lightheadedness, and flushed skin. Thirst is a poor indication of when to take a drink. By the time you are thirsty, the damage may have already been done. You'll be surprised how refreshing it is and how much better you'll feel at the end of the day if you drink and drink often, even if you are not thirsty.

I recommend carrying two to three quarts of water per person per day. Men require more water than women. If you don't like to drink plain water carry a sport drink or take a powdered sport drink mix to add to your water bottle.

CHAD OLSEN

∘∘∘ **95** ∘∘∘

There is no rule of thumb about how far is too far to backpack a float tube. I rarely pack a float tube more than four or five miles if it involves any elevation gain, but many anglers I know hike over ten miles with their belly boat. I recommend buying a scaled-down float tube, not one with all the bells and whistles. Eliminate any extra weight, because you will have to be carrying fins and waders, too.

Many float-tube manufacturers now make bladders which can be inflated by mouth. If I have only a mile or two to hike, I strap my float tube, fully inflated, to my pack, and walk in. For longer or tougher hikes, I partially deflate my float tube, and later inflate it with a bike pump. Hand pumps take forever to inflate a float tube, at least a half hour, so be prepared to go at it awhile. Manufacturers also make several versions they claim can be packed into the high country fully inflated, and come with an array of belts and straps; many fit over your shoulders and back like a backpack. Look into it if this sounds like it is for you. Just make sure your don't have a lot of weight on your shoulders by the end of your hike.

JEROME BUTLER

∘∘∘ 96 ∘∘∘

Don't Accidentally Spread Whirling Disease

Whirling disease is known to exist in the Rocky Mountain states and a few states on both coasts. Biologists now believe that whirling disease (WD) has caused the decline of trout numbers on rivers managed for naturally reproducing wild trout.

The disease is thought to have originated in Europe, where it was discovered in 1893. It made its way to the United

States in 1956 through fish-culture operations. Whirling disease is an infection affecting immature salmonids (trout and salmon), and is caused by a protozoan parasite, Myxobolus cerebralis. The parasite damages cartilage surrounding the brain, causing head and skeletal deformities. The deformity can pinch nerves, causing the fish to swim with a whirling motion, thus the name. Affected trout may be more susceptible to other causes of death, including water quality, stress, and predation.

Myxobolus cerebralis is transmitted by a spore. It requires a secondary host. When an infected fish dies and decomposes, the spores are released and are then eaten by a secondary host, the tubifex worm. New spores are produced in the worm and released into the water. There, they can infect trout by attaching to the gills or from eating infected tubifex worms. Other than being aware of the problem, is there anything anglers can do about the problem? Fly-fishers may not be able to eradicate WD, but there are ways to avoid inadvertently spreading the disease.

After fishing waters with known infection, sanitize any equipment that had contact with the water. Thoroughly rinse waders and fly-lines in clean water to wash away spores. Be certain to do this before fishing uninfected waters.

Avoid overstressing trout when playing them. Net and release fish as quickly as possible. Handle fish carefully. Barbless hooks make it easier to unhook a trout without removing it from the water. Anglers should consider not fishing places where trout are spawning. They are stressed enough by WD and don't need additional strain. Don't try to enhance the fishing in other places by transplanting fish. Stay informed. Wildlife departments periodically release information to the public and as new ways arise to combat the problem, they will pass it on to anglers.

AL MARLOWE

∘∘∘ **97** ∘∘∘

It's Called Fly-Fishing, Not Fly-Casting

One fine evening, a few summers ago, my friend Wayne and I found ourselves standing shoulder to shoulder in a veritable picket line of others, casting without much success at fish rising over against the far shore of Hazel Flats on the Willowemoc. It was difficult, in the gathering dusk, to determine precisely what was hatching—most likely, the small caddis known to Catskill fishers as the shad fly—but the fish were feeding rather avidly.

At one point, having managed to cast some sort of cat's cradle into my leader, I backed up into shallower water to keep the current from pulling the knot tighter as I struggled to pull it apart. Only then did I notice the fellow who was fishing behind the picket line.

He was standing in knee-deep water about midway between the near shore and the line of flailing fly-casters. How he managed to avoid all those backcasts, I don't know, but he was doing very well indeed, making short casts parallel to the shore, getting strikes on roughly every other cast. During the time it took me to disentangle my Gordian knot, I watched that one fellow catch and release more trout than all the other anglers combined. For their part, they were oblivious to what was going on behind them, concentrating instead on those trout feeding against the far shore. Just as I had been.

All the rest of us had violated one of the first principles of sound fly-fishing:

Never cast over water you can wade, or wade through water you can fish.

In our eagerness to get fishing, we often subvert our primary purpose: presenting flies to fish. So intent are we on fishing the obvious lies, we overlook the subtler ones. We blunder right through fish that are resting or feeding in the shallows. We spook fish in the runs and glides by casting over them to reach the deeper pools and undercut banks. We fish a riffle as if it had only one fish-holding pocket. We must learn to do better.

If you can't curb your overeagerness through willpower alone, try this: instead of stringing up your rod as soon as you climb out of the car and into your waders, wait until you reach the water. And stop several feet short of the bank, so your presence won't scare off the nearest fish. Study the water carefully before selecting and tying on a fly.

Make that first cast a short one. And the second. And the third. By the time you have fished your way to within a short cast's distance of that prime lie you ordinarily would have assaulted first, you will probably have raised, maybe even caught, a fish. Maybe even two. Or three.

GARY SOUCIE

∘∘∘ **98** ∘∘∘

Fly-Fishing Down Under

When preparing for my first trip to New Zealand, I read that fly-lines for the country's crystal-clear waters must be as drab as possible—battleship gray, murky olive, and so on. I purchased several lines designed for New Zealand, since most of mine were peach or light buckskin. The guides I fished with on both islands informed me that they are happy with almost any color except bright red, yellow, or any other gaudy, fluorescent color. So take your regular lines and apply the savings toward an exciting "Heli Flyout" into the backcountry while you're in Kiwiland.

Not every cast in New Zealand's waters need be a 40-foot delicate dry-fly presentation. Nymphs tied with tungsten beads are highly effective in New Zealand's streams where trout frequently feed along the bottom in deep currents. The concentrated weight of a tungsten bead crash-dives a fly quickly in situations where the probability of drag makes it difficult to cast far enough above a fish to allow an ordinary beadhead to reach the necessary depth.

Shorter casts are also easier and more accurate in wind (and there are times when wind can be a serious problem down under). So make sure to take along some tungsten beadhead Hare's Ear and Pheasant Tail nymphs.

WILLIAM BLACK

∘∘∘ **99** ∘∘∘

Ultralight Fly-Fishing Gear

Ultralight fly-fishing gear is becoming more and more popular. Fishing with a 1-weight rod is challenging and tests the skills of the more advanced angler. Fly-fishing with ultralight gear can be a lot of fun as long as we don't overestimate our equipment or our abilities. The last thing any of us want to see is a fish expire because we played it too long, a common problem for the beginning ultralight fly-rodder. Most of us wouldn't go after steel-head with an 8-weight. Nor would we receive much pleasure in fishing for 8-inch wild fish with an 8-weight rod. But it is possible to fish and catch big fish on light fly tackle and, in fact, to release these big fish successfully so they can live to fight another day. Learn first how to play and land smaller fish on ultralight fly tackle before moving on to larger fish.

One of the disadvantages to using ultralight gear in the west is that you will encounter many windy days. 1-, 2-, and 3-weight rods were not designed to cast in moderate to heavy winds, although with some practice, it can be accomplished. And even though it can be done—and note that casting an ultralight rod in heavy wind is not a pretty sight—I would not want to cast a #4 mylar minnow with a 1- or 2-weight.

Ultralight tackle does have advantages over conventional fly tackle. The lighter gear allows the fish to be livelier. Ultralight rods also make fishing small streams more fun, put more fight in the small fish. In spring creek situations, the ultralight gear places the fly on the water with an incredible lightness, delicacy. Many times, I have observed fish that when cast to with a 4-weight scattered. With a one-weight, they never flinched when the fly softly landed on the water. If you haven't already, you owe it to yourself to get your hands on a 1-, 2- or 3-weight fly-rod outfit and have yourself some ultralight fun.

LOREN BRADLEY

Hatology 101

When it comes to fly angling tackle, there is *nothing* more important than your hat. Scientists have estimated than nearly 50 percent of all unsuccessful fishing trips can be attributed to someone's wearing the wrong hat.

Scoff you may, but the government has spent millions on the scientific research of Hatology (the study of hats in relation to angling) and have shown the findings are just as valid as those as any found in the government-sponsored science of Underology (the study of thermal underwear in relation to angling) or even their sacred cow: Spendology (the study to determine how much money they can spend on studies before the taxpayers get wise).

Hatology is not only relevant but a prerequisite to successful angling. If you can't pass Hatology, you might as well take up tennis.

As an example, let's take a look at my fishing partner, Stern McFurder. I've fished with Stern for a good many years now and have gathered conclusive evidence that he does, in fact, catch significantly great numbers of trout when wearing one style of hat as opposed to another. As a student of Hatology, you pay attention to this kind of stuff.

Last summer, Stern showed up for one fishing trip wearing something other than his usual hat. "For cripes sake, Stern!" I said. "What the blue-blazes are you doing wearing that thing? You know darned good and well you never catch trout unless you're sporting your farmer-green baseball cap. Are you trying to skunk the entire trip?"

Well now, Stern was never one to let objections from his fellow anglers dictate his choice of fishing headgear, so my comment was dismissed with a shrug and a verbal reply that I can't repeat without being censored. As I predicted, though, he flogged and flogged the water mercilessly hour after hour and caught nary a fish. Even then, would Stern accept the obvious fact that his hat was acting as a fish repellent? No. He just kept on casting and casting and not catching a fish—

none right after none. And as I also predicted, the rest of us didn't catch any fish
either.

That is the thorny part of the Wrong
Hat Syndrome. There is much better
than odd chance that wearing the wrong
hat will not only jinx your own fishing
endeavors but will most likely put the fish
down for hundreds of miles around and
muck up everyone else's chances too. If
this fact is ever made public to your fellow fishers, the probability of a streamside mob action increases tenfold and the
outcome can get just a bit messy. The tar
and feathering of a foul-hatted angler is a
terribly traumatic ordeal.

"I'm telling you straight, Stern, you've
got to get rid of that thing," I demanded.

"No way!" he insisted. "I'm going to
start reeling 'em in any minute now. I'm
sure my luck will change. Just as soon as
I get the tar out of my reel and—hey, I
think this is a size twenty Coachman
Brown hackle feather! Told you I'd get
lucky."

Stern was feigning false pleasure over
the discovery of the dry-fly hackle mixed
in with the tar, but this observer did not

fall for the obvious ploy. Stern was indeed beginning to have second thoughts about his choice of fishing hat. Nothing short of a rusted wheel cover had been caught in twelve hours of hard fishing and the river level was starting to drop, as if it were cringing at Stern's hat.

At the end of the fifteenth hour, Stern conceded the inevitable and agreed to change hats. The mob that gathered to show a new-design slip knot removed the rope from his neck and made Stern sign a contract that stated he would wear only his farmer-green baseball cap while angling and the trouble-making genuine coonskin cap (complete with a badly shedding raccoon tail) would only be worn at costume parties, at midnight, during a total eclipse of the moon.

Just as soon as Stern switched hats, the bite was on and the river level returned to normal.

Obviously, the choice of hats is critical, so the safest bet is to keep with the usual bill of fare when it comes to angler-domes. Baseball caps with assorted advertising for rod or tackle companies, beer, tractor, or fly-shops are acceptable.

A baseball cap that indicates a baseball team is not recommended, but one with a football team logo is fine. Cowboy hats festooned with assorted crown-bands of leather, feather, or barbed wire are okay, but only when fishing in Montana.

Such attire is not something we'd like to see on the bonefish of Christmas Island. You can only wear silly hats when fishing for bonefish. Deerstalker (à la Sherlock Holmes) and those ever-popular fish-through-the-head hats have not been proved to chase off fish, so if you're inclined—go ahead on. If you have the guts to wear them, we have the guts to accept them. These hats will not have a negative effect on your fishing excursions—your love life maybe—but not your fishing.

In the event you do decide to venture out of the norm there are just a few items to keep in mind. The use of polo helmets, cadet caps, or British pith helmets is strictly forbidden. This is because:

(1) Your hat must be able to be easily blown off your head and be held aloft while you attempt to grab it for no less than 30 feet at a stretch. This frustrating

process must continue for a minimum of fifteen minutes or until the hat sinks like a rock in the riffle.

(2) A hat must be constructed of a material that can be torn to shreds by blackberry bushes, low-hanging oak branches, or tall grass. It must, however, be constructed of a material that makes it impossible to remove the miscast Muddler without a pocketknife and life-threatening puncture wounds.

Scientific research has proved time and time again that the only thing worse than wearing the wrong fishing hat is the negligent act of not wearing a hat at all. To attempt to cast without wearing a hat is criminal and simply unthinkable. Your "lucky" fishing hat is even more essential to your success than a bottle of shrimp oil or an electric hook sharpener.

If you are still not clear as to which hat is right for you, just rely on you own natural angler observations. Pick a hat that looks like something you might wish to wear outdoors. Place it on your head and eye yourself in the mirror. If you can hold that smirk for forty-two seconds or longer, you've got yourself a lucky fishing hat.

But if your take your spouse to the hospital to be heavily tranquilized for hysterical, nonstop laughter that erupted when you tried on the hat—you'll know you don't have a mere fishing hat but a genuine angler's crown. Good luck and good hatting!

GENE TRUMP

°°° **101** °°°

The Backcountry

After obsessively pursuing fly-fishing for many years, my choicest tip to other paramours would not be a matter of tackle or technique, but more like a philosophy of trip-taking to maximize your satisfactions from this sport we love.

In the course of a fly-fisher's natural evolution, we gradually grow from intimidating struggle with the basics to catching little fish to catching lots of fish to catching big fish to catching ever-more-difficult fish to record bluewater fish, to, I believe, eventually not caring much whether we catch fish at all, provided we can simply be here now in the beautiful places that fish happen to be for their own sake, for the sake of cleansing and renewing our souls. In a word, the ultimate destination of a fly-fisher's maturity is *wilderness*.

Over the years, I've caught many big fish; at least as many, I've decided, as any man really needs. I do think back fondly on a few monsters, but what I value most in all this experience is not so much testing myself against the fish as against the natural environments they live in. To me, the deepest satisfactions in fly-fishing come not from fish per se but from multi-day plunges into the wilderness back-country where, by carrying my own weight on my own back, and depending entirely on my own resources, I have the best chance to feel like a natural part of the process that put it all here in the first place.

In this light, fly-fishing is not an end in itself, but only a means (although the best I know of) to experience the godly oneness and perfection of things, including ourselves in all our blundering banality. For me, fly-fishing has finally become not so much a destination for sport, as a venue for discovery and acceptance of self.

Trouble is, we often come to this realization too late in life to think we can do much about it. Our hair thins, our bellies sag, our feet ache, our spirit is compromised by the declines of the body and the demands of the "real" world. We know the real world beckons—the natural world in which we are only a visitor—but increasingly come to think it beyond our reach. My advice is to make such opportunities now, since you're obviously not getting any younger. Plunge as deep and as long into wilderness as you can possibly afford, as often as possible, before you get too old to rationally consider it. You will be rewarded with experiences and memories no fish trophies could equal.

We are blessed in America with abundant wilderness reserves, but they are under constant assault from the forces of exploitative "development" and corporate welfare queens, so taste them while they still exist, while you still can. Read books, study maps, respect your fantasies, and take focused steps to enact them. Personally, I believe backpacking the finest way to enjoy the wilderness experience, but cars, airplanes, horses, and rafts will also get you there. The point is, do it now, before it's too late, or rather before you believe you can't do it anymore, at which point, you won't.

HUGH GARDNER

∘∘∘ **102** ∘∘∘

Guides Come in All Shapes and Sizes

One of the most difficult aspects of fishing, one of the more unexplained mysteries of the sport, one of the things they just don't teach you at casting school or fly-tying class, is how to hire a fly-fishing guide. How much should one cost? How much should I tip? What do I do if I don't like the guide, if I don't catch fish, if I hook his ear?

Guides come in all shapes and sizes, in a variety of demeanors and attitudes and life experiences. No two anglers agree on exactly what makes a good guide. Is the best guide the one who puts you into a lot of fish? Is it the guide who takes the time to teach you the skills to make you a better angler? Is it the guide who is interesting, validates the trip with information and personality, the one who serves up a good lunch? Or is it the guide who can handle a boat, stays all day on the water, has a name reputation? I suggest that what makes a good guide is what you believe makes a good guide—probably a combination of many of the above traits.

Here are a few tips to make hiring a guide a less disturbing proposition, finding a guide that fits your criteria, then insuring you get the most out of the experience:

- Tell the guide what kind of fishing you like. Say if you want to fish for trophy trout, if you like lakes, if you want to try to catch a wild trout off the beaten path, learn how to cast better, and so on.

- Call around and compare services, prices, whether or not you like the persons you talk with. Ask friends about their times out with guide services, outfitters, fly-shops. Read magazines, newsletters, check with trout-fishing organizations.

- Share with the guide what equipment you own, and ask if it fits the type of water you will be fishing. Don't be afraid to ask the guide if you will be fishing mostly with nymphs or dry flies, if you need to bring special equipment, what the typical strategies are for fishing these waters. If you like fishing at dusk, tell the guide. Topflight guides want to please you and will gladly accommodate your desires. If they won't do that, find another guide.

- Ask guides questions, plain and simple. I won't say there are no dumb questions but it won't be the first time they have heard them. Ask them how long they plan to keep you out. How long will you be on the water, in the boat? Does the boat have a knee rest? Do they provide rain gear? What kind of boat is it? Will they provide flies? Lunch? Transportation? You would be surprised how these services vary from guide to guide. Many guides now charge for flies.

- The guide should not fish. You and whoever else is a client should fish.

- Many guides now ask for payment up front. Tip guides at the end of the day if you think they have been professional, have done their job of trying to help you have a quality day of fishing. Don't judge it just on how many fish you caught.

∘ Try to listen to the guide. Sounds easy, but you'd be surprised how difficult it is to teach someone who nods in agreement but continues to fail to master a new skill. All boat guides can be readily identified by the numbers of scars on their ears and hands from errant casts by backseat anglers. The guide takes out fishers daily and usually has a reason to take the time to tell you something—it might even save you from an accident. So listen up.

∘ Remember that guides are not magicians and they are sometimes hampered by weather conditions, water conditions, your lousy fishing abilities. Try as they may, they may not always be able to put you into record numbers of record size fish. Don't make fishing with a guide a numbers game. If you go out with a solid guide and don't come away with more skills, with more information, with a feeling that he or she did everything possible to maximize your day (or days), then you haven't done your part. There is a definite symbiotic relationship between client and guide.

Many times, you are a student, the guide the teacher. As your skills grow, you will more often find yourself a peer. But fishing on someone else's home waters always means that they know the intricacies of the stream or lake better than you.

One of the most important aspects of success on the water with a professional guide is by being honest with yourself. Many guides plan the day's trip based on their assessment of your skills, on the information you provide them. Many will ask you over the phone about your casting skills, about how often you fish, how long you have been fly-fishing, and so on. If you deceive them because you are afraid to be embarrassed, you are likely to end up on more challenging water, catching few fish, having wasted an opportunity to learn from a professional angler. It's your money, your time.

I suggest being up front and honest with the guide. You won't be the first beginner the guide has taken to the stream. If you fish every now and again, but like to think you are better than you are, humble yourself a bit and fess up. You will learn more about casting, tying knots, choosing flies, reading water, landing fish than you ever would if you pretended you already knew everything.

And what do you do if you get a guide who is obviously unprofessional, has a bad attitude, is a smart-ass, or is incompetent? Many guides are associated with fly-shops, or have bosses. Take your complaint to a higher source. Talk to the owner. Be honest about what you expected. I think hiring a poor guide is a rare thing—bad guides don't last long in this business—but it occasionally happens.

MAC BROWN

°°° **103** °°°

Fly-Fishing with Children

At five and a half years old, my son Ben had sat through so many fishing trips without having any success or fun that he decided it wasn't worth his time. "Don't get too close to the river, don't get in my tackle box, don't throw rocks, and don't let the fly drift into that tree," went my array of commands on any of our trips. What usually followed was my plea, "Please don't cry, Ben."

It was with the help of some panfish (bluegill in this case), that Ben changed his mind about fly-fishing. It sounds stupid, but perch can help create a little fly-fishing buddy. Children have short attention spans and they need to catch fish soon after they hit the water. Sunfish and panfish fill the bill. These little guys will usually hit anything that hits the water.

You can find these small fish almost everywhere, from farm ponds a mile out of town to great lakes to small streams; they can survive in almost any kind of water. Not even long trips or early morning ventures can put a crimp on a kid's enjoyment of feeling the electric tug of a colorful panfish at the end of the line. The panfish live close to the shore, so a kid's casting limitations don't often come into play. And most panfish are not picky about lousy presentations either. And rocks tossed in the water rarely put down a panfish.

Children can observe the water, learn about the fish, the insects, the fly patterns, all in good time, because a kid catching fish learns a lot easier and more rapidly than a bored kid tackling trout and tough water.

Most panfish can be handled with curiosity and rough little hands without much fear that the fish will be harmed before releasing it. On light fly-tackle, panfish can put up quite a hearty fight for the youngsters. Perfect lesson for learning how to play and land a fish.

Panfish may not be the fish of choice for most anglers, but for teaching young anglers the art of fly-fishing, they can lend a fin in showing the merits of the sport. Fishing for panfish might also take you back to your childhood, back when fishing was done more for fun than sport.

TERRY MOORE

∘∘∘ **104** ∘∘∘

The Six-Pack Rule

A fishing buddy by the name of Mike Albers once told me about this excellent rule-of-thumb, which is hardly scientific but highly effective in locating lightly fished trout waters. It has served me well with fishing waters that are near heavily populated areas and that get a healthy dose of stocker rainbows and thus local bait dunkers. Say what you will about the latter, they can be efficient predators.

When fishing streams like the one I describe, try locating a stretch that heads away from the nearest roadside access and walk either up or downstream from it. If the stream in question veers off into a heavily wooded area with primitive trails, or into a box canyon, this is an ideal situation to invoke the six-pack rule. You see, most anglers have a hard time decid-ing just how far to walk away from the local river campground or parking area in their quest for "virgin" waters and wild fish. How many times have you decided, "This time I'm gonna hike at least thirty minutes upstream before rigging my fly," only to lose all resolve at the first sign of a nice riffle or dry-fly pool? The problem is that we don't have a true methodology to follow.

My buddy Mike suggests counting empty beer cans along the stream or path. Some call them "beer sign"—a sure indicator that some local predators have been marauding in the area. If you have the patience and discipline to locate these "beer signs," you will discover that as you approach the magic number six, paths become less marked, branches begin to whack you in the head more firmly as you make your way through the woods, the bugs get thicker, and even the pools seem to look bigger. Enjoy the fishing, and please pack out those cans if you don't mind.

MANUEL MONASTERIO

The Contributors

Ed Adams
Ed Adams Flyfishing Guide Service
  Guide, instructor
P.O. Box 428
Questa, NM 87556
(505) 586-1512

Al Beatty
Freelance writer, national marketing director for
  Whiting Farms, owner of BT's Fly Fishing
  Products
3020 Secor Ave.
Bozeman, MT 59715-6150
(406) 585-0745
E-mail: albeatty@alpinenet.net
http://www.btsflyfishing.com

Dr. William Black
Author of many books including Flyfishing the
  Rockies
Albuquerque, NM

Loren Bradley
Troutback Guide Service
Professional guide, outdoor writer
P.O. Box 344
942 E. Maricopa Drive
Springerville, AZ 85938
(520) 333-5377

Harry Briscoe
Owner of Hexagraph Rod Company
9919 Hornpipe Lane
Houston, TX 77080
(800) 870-4211

Mac Brown, Ph.D.
Professor at Western Carolina, guide and fly-
  casting instructor
Author of numerous fly-fishing articles
Owner of McCleod's Highland Flyfishing
191 Wesser Heights Drive
Bryson City, NC 28713
(828) 488-8975

Barrie Bush
Guide, instructor, wholesaler
Santa Fe Fly-Fishing School
P.O. Box 22957
Santa Fe, NM 87502
505-986-3913

Jerome Butler
Guide, instructor, Fishing Manager of Main
   Street Outfitters
501 Main Street
Fort Worth, TX 76102
(817) 332-76102

Jim Butler
Editor of Fly Rod & Reel
P.O. Box 370
Camden, ME 04843
(800) 766-1670

Doug Camp
Owner of Willows Bed & Breakfast
Professional guide and lecturer
NDCBU 6560
Taos, NM 87571
(800) 525-8267

Paul Canada

Professional outdoor writer

Contributing editor for Bass Pro Shops: Outdoor
World

2312 Brockbank St.

Irving, TX 75062

(972) 252-1612

Jay Cassell

Articles Editor for Sports Afield

250 W. 55th Street

New York, NY 10019

(212) 649-4302

Brian Chan

Outdoor writer, fisheries biologist, author of
Flyfishing Strategies for Stillwaters

P.O. Box 374

Kamloops, B.C. V2C 5K9

E-mail: bmchan@mail.netshop.net

Ralph and Lisa Cutter

Freelance writers, instructors, authors of Sierra
Trout Guide

Owners of California School of Flyfishing

P.O. Box 8212

11775 Alder Dr., Truckee, CA 96162

(916) 587-7005

Jerral Derryberry

Professional landscape and fly-fishing painter,
photographer, freelance writer

3752 Seguin Drive

Dallas, TX 75220

(214) 352-2773

E-mail: Derryberry@Juno.com

Marcos Enriquez

Fishing Manager, Orvis Dallas, guide, fly-casting
instructor

10720 Preston Road

Dallas, TX 75230

(214) 265-1600

Hugh Gardner, Ph.D.

Former editor of Rocky Mountain Streamside

Contributing editor for The Angling Report

Producer/director of Incredible Journey of the
Greenback Cutthroat *film*

Author of many fly-fishing destination articles

P.O. Box 227

Idledale, CO 80453-0227

(303) 697-5876

Terry Gunn

Co-owner of Lees Ferry Anglers Fly Shop
Noted fly-casting instructor and fly-fishing guide
HC 67-Box 2
Marble Canyon, AZ 86036
(800) 962-9755
http://www.leesferry.com
E-mail: tgunn@leesferry.com

Wendy Hanvold-Gunn

Co-owner of Lees Ferry Anglers Fly Shop
Noted fly-casting instructor and fly-fishing guide
HC 67-Box 2
Marble Canyon, AZ 86036
(800) 962-9755

Dave Hughes

Freelance writer, author of several books, videos
including Western Hatches, Western
Streamside Guide, Yellowstone River and Its
Angling, Strategies for Streams Series, Big
Indian Creek
2355 SW Cedar #12
Portland, OR 97205

Craig Kautsch
Owner, Main Street Outfitters, instructor
501 Main Street
Fort Worth, TX 76102
(817) 332-4144
E-mail: kautsch@flash.net

Mark Kovach
Professional fly-fishing instructor, fly-fishing guide
737 Thayer Avenue
Silver Spring, MD 20910
(301) 588-8742

Mel Krieger
Noted fly-casting instructor, teacher
Author of many books and articles on fly-fishing
Owner of Mel Krieger School of Flyfishing
790 27th Avenue
San Francisco, CA 94121
(415) 752-0192

Lyndon Lampert
Head guide at Dan's Fly Shop, publishes western
  guide directory, fly-tyer
P.O. Box 14
Lake City, CO 81235
(970) 944-2732
E-mail: lampert@gunnison.com

Tim Linehan

*Guide, freelance writer, owner of guide service on
  Kootenai River*

472 Upper Ford Road

Troy, MT 59935

(406) 295-4872

Al Marlowe

Freelance writer, author of Flyfishing Colorado
  River, *photographer, guide*

P.O. Box 2243

Evergreen, CO 80439

(303) 670-7219

Paul Marriner

*Freelance writer, author of many articles and
  books*

103 Mader's Cove Rd., RR1

Mahone Bay, Nova Scotia, Canada NS
  B0J 2E0

E-mail: pmarr@tallships.istar.ca

Craig Martin
Author and editor, Flyfishing Northern New
    Mexico, Flyfishing Southern Colorado
465 Grand Canyon Drive
Los Alamos, NM 87544
(505) 672-1962
E-mail: cmartin@rt66.com

Craig Mathews and John Juracek
*Owners of Blue Ribbon Flies Fly Shop, freelance
    writers, authors of several books, professional
    guides and fly-tyers*
P.O. Box 1037
West Yellowstone, MT 59758
(406) 646-9365

Ken Medling
Co-owner, River Maps Company
Coauthor, Flyfishing Northeastern New Mexico
Professional outdoor writer, columnist,
    photographer
3918 Linda
Amarillo, TX 79109
(806) 356-9578
E-mail: kbuffalo@arn.net

Manuel Monasterio

Owner, guide, Reel Life Fly Shops, Santa Fe and Albuquerque

100 San Mateo Blvd., NE Suite 10

Albuquerque, NM 87110

(505) 268-1693

E-mail: 74724.1674@CompuServe.com

Terry Moore

Freelance writer, Outdoors editor for Amarillo Globe News

900 Harrison

Amarillo, TX 79166

(806) 345-3308

Skip Morris

Freelance writer, professional fly-tyer, author of many books including The Custom Graphite Fly Rod, FlyTying Made Clear and Simple, The Art of Tying the Nymph, The Art of Tying the Dry Fly, Tying Foam Flies, Concise Handbook of Fly Tying, *and producer of several videos including* The Art of Tying the Nymph.

P.O. Box 65140

Port Ludlow, WA 98365

(360) 437-2717

Harry Murray
Freelance writer of books and articles
Professional guide and instructor
Owner of Murray's Fly Shop
P.O. Box 156, 121 Main St.
Edinburg, VA
(800) 984-4895

Bob Newman
Freelance writer, guide, author of several books
    including North American Flyfishing
2154 Sherri Mar St.
Longmont, CO 80501
(303) 774-9690
E-mail: bobnew@rmi.net

Chad Olsen
Greater Yellowstone Flyfishers
Guide, freelance writer, owner of Greater
    Yellowstone Flyfishers
8471 Lupine Lane
Bozeman, MT 59718
(406) 838-2468

Dan Powell

Instructor

Woody Creek, CO

E-mail: dandorth@aol.com

Ray Sasser

Outdoor Sports Editor, Dallas Morning News

Author of many fishing articles, several books

Dallas, TX

Jeff and Cyndie Schmitt

Professional outdoor writers

*Former president, Trout Unlimited Guadalupe
    Chapter*

2512 Star Grass Circle

Austin, TX 78745

(512) 282-6016

E-mail: SWPKO5A@prodigy.com

Ed Shenk

*Legendary instructor for Allenberry School of
    Flyfishing, author, professional flytyer*

500 Franklin Street

Carlisle, PA 17013

(717) 243-2679

Marty Sherman

Co-owner of River Graphics with his wife, Joyce.
    They specialize in catalog, book, newsletter
    and brochure production and design.
3808 SW Huber, Portland, OR 97219.
(503) 244-4109
E-mail: jsherman@teleport.com

Gary Soucie

Editor of American Angler, *author of* Traveling
    with Fly Rod and Reel, *and* Hook, Line and
    Sinker: The Complete Angler's Guide to
    Terminal Tackle *and editor of* Home Waters:
    A Fly-Fishing Anthology
126 North Street
Bennington, VT 05201
(802) 447-1518

Jim Teeny

Owner of Teeny Nymph Lines, Writer, Instructor
Teeny Nymph Company
P.O. Box 989
Gresham, OR 97030
(503) 667-6602

Tom Theus

Public Speaker with Joan Whitlock Speaker's
  Bureau
Conducts Fly-casting Schools
Lecturer on both Saltwater and Freshwater
  Flyfishing
114 Pinebrook Drive
Boiling Springs, SC 29316
(864) 599-7402

Doc Thompson

Professional guide, freelance writer, columnist
Owner, High Country Anglers
P.O. 252
Cimarron, NM 87714
(505) 376-9220

Stephen Trammel

Editor of Rocky Mountain Streamside
Author of several fly-fishing articles
5026 East Geddes Ave.
Littleton, CO 80102-2447
(303) 694-1034
E-mail: Steve.Trammel@frontier.pidwights.com

Gene Trump

*American Angler fly-tying columnist, freelance
writer, cartoonist, author of several books*

P.O. Box 1905

Corvalis, OR 97339-1905

E-mail: trumpg@ProAxis.com

Hartt Wixom

Editor, freelance writer, author of Utah Fishing
and Hunting Guide

1730 Willowbrook Drive

Provo, UT 84604-1393

(801) 374-0054